Make Play

ROCK™

PUT PRETENDING INTO YOUR CHILD'S PLAY

Make Play R.O.C.K.™ – Put Pretending into Your Child's Play
Booklet 3
By Elaine Weitzman and Lisa Drake

© Hanen Early Language Program, 2015.

The Hanen Program, The Hanen Centre, the Parent-Child Logo and Make Play R.O.C.K. are trademarks owned by Hanen Early Language Program.

All rights reserved. No part of this booklet may be reproduced by mimeograph or by any other means without the written permission of the publisher. This booklet may not be translated, in part or in whole, without written permission from the publisher.

Library and Archives Canada
ISBN 978-0-921145-50-9

Copies of this and other booklets in the series may be ordered from the publisher:
The Hanen Centre
1075 Bay Street, Suite 515
Toronto, ON, M5S 2B1

Telephone: (416) 921-1073
Fax: (416) 921-1225
E-mail: info@hanen.org
www.hanen.org

Parts of this booklet were adapted from:
More Than Words®: A Parent's Guide to Building Interaction and Language Skills for Children with Autism Spectrum Disorder or Social Communication Difficulties by Fern Sussman (2012), a Hanen Centre publication and *Take Out the Toys: Building Early Toy Play for Children with Autism Spectrum Disorder and Social Communication Difficulties* by Fern Sussman and Elaine Weitzman (2014), a Hanen Centre publication

Photography: Tania Cannarella
Additional Photography: iStockPhoto
Design: Matt Monaco
Editor: Andrea Lynn Koohi
Printed in Canada by Transcontinental Interglobe Inc.

Table of Contents

Introduction to Booklet 3: Put Pretending into Your Child's Play	1
Part 1: All About Pretend Play	8
Part 2: Your Child's Stage of Play and Next Steps in Pretend Play	18
Part 3: Build Pretend Play Within Playful Interactions: Follow Your Child's Lead and R.O.C.K.	28
Part 4: Real Life Examples	48
Sample Pretend Play Plan	60
My Child's Pretend Play Plan	62

Introduction to Booklet 3: Put Pretending into Your Child's Play

Welcome to Booklet 3 of the Make Play R.O.C.K.™ series! *Put Pretending into Your Child's Play* will give you the tools to help your child develop more advanced **pretend play skills** – skills that are closely linked with the development of language, social, and emotional skills.

This booklet contains many practical ideas and excellent examples of how to first Follow Your Child's Lead to establish a back and forth, enjoyable interaction with your child. Then it explains how to R.O.C.K your child's play so you can go directly from reading the booklet to building your child's pretend play, using the strategies you have just read about. Read on to find out how to make pretend play with your child playful and productive!

The power of play

Play is as essential to a child's life as eating and sleeping. Your child learns something from every play experience. When he picks up a toy train and spins its wheels, he learns that he can make things happen. When he hears you say, "That train's wheels go round and round," he discovers that objects and actions have names. And when he holds a toy stethoscope to his sister's chest, pretending to be a doctor, he has a chance to experience what it feels like to be someone else.

Through play children learn about themselves and the world around them. Everything that your child needs to learn – social skills, vocabulary, language skills and even how to solve problems – can be learned through play.

When a child has difficulty learning to play

Learning to play doesn't happen easily for all children. Children with developmental challenges such as autism spectrum disorder (ASD) and other social communication difficulties have a challenging time learning to play. It's hard for them to pay attention to and copy what other people are doing, which means that they aren't learning play skills from their parents and other children the way typically developing children do. Some children with ASD do the same single action with a toy over and over again (for example, lifting the dumper of a dump truck up and down), resulting in play that is repetitive and not very creative. Children on the autism spectrum aren't naturally flexible thinkers. That's why pretend play, which requires them to imagine a different world from the real one—for example, a world in which they are firefighters or dads—can be especially difficult for them.

When a child's play skills are not developing as expected, his opportunities for learning are limited and so are his opportunities to have fun. That's why it is important to take action early. Children with ASD and other social communication difficulties need help with play so they can develop the many skills that grow from everyday play experiences.

“Children with ASD and other social communication difficulties need help with play so they can develop the many skills that grow from everyday play experiences.”

Your child's play skills

Think about how your child plays and answer the following questions:

- Does your child look like he's having fun when he plays (does he laugh and smile)?
- Does your child look at you or talk to you when he plays with a toy?
- Does your child copy what you do with toys?
- Does your child play with a variety of toys?
- Does your child play in different ways with the same toy (for example, build a tower with his blocks and pretend a block is a ball or a car)?
- Does your child like to play with other children?

If you answered "no" to any of these questions, the *Make Play R.O.C.K.* booklet series will give you the tools to help your child improve his play skills in these areas. If your child doesn't play with a variety of toys, is stuck playing the same way all the time or can't use his imagination to figure out what else he can do with his toys, he's missing out on opportunities to develop his language and thinking skills. And he's also missing out on a lot of fun when playing with you and others.

You can help your child learn to play

The good news is that you can help your child develop more advanced play skills *and* ensure that he has fun while he's learning. The *Make Play R.O.C.K.* booklet series offers easy, practical strategies for helping your child play in more flexible and creative ways and learn more while doing it. The strategies in *Make Play R.O.C.K.*, which are based on up-to-date research, do not involve teaching play through drills or following a prescribed curriculum. They simply enable you to build your child's play skills in all kinds of typical play activities that will be joyful and fun for you both.

What results can you expect from using the *Make Play* ROCK booklets?

As you start using the suggestions in *Make Play R.O.C.K.*, you should see that your child is paying more attention to you and interacting with you more often. When this happens, he will probably start copying the new play skills you show him and will begin to use his toys differently. If your child has more advanced play skills, with a little coaching from you, he will discover more creative ways to play. He will also come to realize that playing with other children can be fun once he knows what to do.

Much depends on how often you use the strategies and how much fun your child has when you and he play together. Each child is different, and some ideas will work better for your child than others. One thing is guaranteed: The more time you spend playing with your child using *Make Play R.O.C.K.* strategies, the more opportunities he'll have to learn to play and interact with you. So read on and get ready to R.O.C.K. your child's play!

"The more time you spend playing with your child using *Make Play R.O.C.K.* strategies, the more opportunities he'll have to learn to play and interact with you."

What's in the *Make Play* ROCK series

Booklet 1: Plan for People Play

Plan for People Play is about helping your child play games in which he learns to take turns back and forth with you, usually without any toys. These "people games" like Row, Row, Row Your Boat and Chase help your child learn critically important turn-taking skills, which he can then transfer to other situations. This booklet helps you identify your child's stage in playing people games and describes how to set up these games so you help him take his turn in the game. There are clear guidelines for playing these games in ways that will make it easier for your child to join in more often with an action, a sound or with words. There is a section with many suggestions for people games that build on your child's preferred activities.

Booklet 2: Take Out the Toys

The *Take Out the Toys* booklet gives you the tools to help your child develop early toy play skills. This early type of play, known as functional play, is an important step on the road to developing more advanced play skills, as well as building social skills. Functional play involves playing with toys in "expected" ways, such as putting shapes into a sorter or building a tower with blocks. This booklet has a play checklist, which helps you identify how your child currently plays with toys. From there, you learn how to expand functional play skills by helping him learn to imitate new play actions using a variety of objects and toys. As your child learns to imitate new and more complex types of functional play, he is not only learning new play skills, but is building the foundation for improved language development.

Booklet 3: Put Pretending into Your Child's Play

The *Put Pretending into Your Child's Play* booklet contains some creative strategies for helping your child develop more advanced pretend play skills. This is especially important for a child who has difficulty using his imagination. Here you'll use a checklist to find your child's stage of pretending, which leads to the use of playful strategies to gently guide him to the next stage of pretend play. You will also learn which pretend play toys are best for your child at each stage of development.

A note on pronouns used in this book

To make the text of this booklet as clear as possible, and to reflect the prevalence of Autism Spectrum Disorder in the population (approximately 3 out of 4 children affected are boys), the pronoun "he" is used when referring to the child. However, both boys and girls are featured in the photos throughout the booklet.

1

All About Pretend Play

In this section, you'll learn why pretend play is important for young children and how it builds on other aspects of early development, such as social and language skills. You'll find out about the development of pretend play in both typically developing children and children on the autism spectrum, and what skills your child needs in order to develop pretend play. Then, you will learn about the four Hanen stages of communication development for children with ASD and at which stage pretend play starts to develop. This information will help you determine whether your child is ready for you to build his pretend play.

Why Pretend Play Is Important

Pretend play is a critically important part of all children's development. When a child pretends to be a chef stirring soup or an astronaut going to the moon, he is gaining social and emotional skills, as well as language, problem-solving and thinking skills.

Pretend play and language skills

Pretend play builds children's **language skills**. When pretending, children use one object to stand for another, making that object a symbol. A block becomes a symbol for a car, a ball becomes an apple and a rocking motion represents riding a horse. Language also involves the use of symbols. The word "apple" represents a red, round fruit and the word "gone" represents something that was there, but is no longer. Therefore, both pretend play and language involve the same underlying ability to represent things symbolically, leading many

experts to believe that pretend play helps children develop language and vice versa.

When children pretend, they often use words and phrases they have heard others use. For example, they copy things they have heard their parents say, such as, "Just one and no more!" They also learn to use language creatively as they pretend to be another person. For example, when pretending to be a doctor, they have to learn to ask health-related questions like, "Where does it hurt?" They also need to talk about treatment and medication as a doctor would, which builds their knowledge and understanding of the world.

Pretend play and social and emotional skills

Pretend play helps develop children's **social and emotional skills** because, as they pretend, they experiment with the different social and emotional roles of life. While pretending, they can explore an experience that is confusing or scary, allowing them to feel more comfortable and prepared for these events.

Pretending to be someone else, like a bus driver or a baby, helps children experience what it is like to "walk in someone else's shoes." Young children have difficulty with the idea of thinking about what others think and they tend to see the world through their own eyes. As they pretend to be someone else, they begin to understand other people's perspectives and how another person might think, talk and feel. Seeing the world from other people's perspectives is a key aspect of early childhood development because it helps children interact effectively with others and make friends.

Pretend play also provides children with a variety of challenges, which builds their problem-solving skills. Whether it's deciding which presents Big Bird should receive at his "birthday party" or how to turn a table into a grocery store checkout, children do a lot of thinking and problem-solving during pretend play, gaining skills that they will use not only in childhood, but throughout their lives.

The Sequence of Pretend Play Development

Let's look at the two stages of pretend play that help us understand how this kind of play develops. First, we see the development of **early pretend play** and then, **later pretend play**.

Early pretend play

Early pretend play looks a lot like functional play, which involves playing with toys in "expected" ways, such as putting shapes into a sorter or building a tower with blocks. In early pretend play, the child still uses an object as it is intended to be used, whether it is a miniature toy or the real thing. He performs an action on himself or he acts on another person or object. For example, he "drinks" from a real size empty cup or he gives a doll a drink from a miniature cup. This is a kind of "reality play" in which the child shows that he recognizes what the object is supposed to be used for, whether it is a real-size or a miniature. Perhaps he sees the miniature as a small but real object. Whatever the case, he pretends with a realistic object, using it just like he uses it in real life.

What makes early pretend play different from functional play is that the child is clearly aware that this is not the "real world." He knows there is no liquid in the cup, yet he pretends to drink. He knows that there is no soup in the pot, yet he continues to stir. This shows that he has moved beyond pure functional play into the area of pretending.

Early pretend play often involves feeding, grooming and daily routines since these are so familiar. A competent early pretender can pretend using many different objects and create pretend sequences, such as stirring a spoon in a pan and then putting the spoon to a doll's mouth.

Later pretend play

Later pretend play requires the child to think at a higher level. At this stage, the child is truly pretending. He no longer needs real or realistic objects in order to pretend. He can pretend that a cardboard box or an empty yoghurt container is a car and he "drives" them along the floor, stopping to get gas and then beeping to tell an imaginary person to get out of the way. His newly-developed imagination enables him to "see" the box or container as a car and he can create a little sequence or story with these objects.

This is a more complex skill because it means the child is using symbols with ease. He can use one object to stand for another even if it looks nothing like the real thing and has no trouble keeping in mind what it really stands for. This ability allows him to use any object to pretend. A block can become a car, a phone, a broom, a brush or a tree. All he needs to do is assign an identity to the object and keep that in his mind.

At the later stage of pretend play, the child can even pretend without an object, imagining that an invisible object is the real thing. He may lick an imaginary ice cream or cut with imaginary scissors by moving his fingers in a cutting motion. Once again, it is the ability to hold the idea in his mind that allows him to play in this creative and imaginative way.

Pretend Play and Children on the Autism Spectrum

Play is one of the major difficulties for children on the autism spectrum, especially pretend play. Many children with autism don't pretend spontaneously. They may enjoy moving trains or cars along a track, but they're unlikely to pretend that someone is driving the car and turn it into a pretend "story." Children on the autism spectrum who do engage in pretend play may not pretend often and their play is usually repetitive and not very varied. Pretend play requires a child to put himself into someone else's shoes and to talk and act as if he is that other person. That's something that children with autism spectrum disorder struggle with.

Once a child with autism has mastered higher levels of functional play (described in booklet 2 of Make Play R.O.C.K.™, *Take Out the Toys*), he is ready to pretend. However, it is harder for children with ASD to make the shift from functional play to pretend play even when their functional play is well-developed. It is not always clear whether children with autism spectrum disorder are unable to engage in pretend play or whether they can, but just don't show it. Studies have shown that when children with autism spectrum disorder receive prompts to perform pretend play, they do. However, even so, they may appear to have less fun and be less playful when they do pretend.

Pretend play is an important skill for children on the autism spectrum because studies show that better pretend play skills in these children at age three and four are associated with better language skills at ages eight and nine . In addition, the more varied and flexible the child's pretend play, the more advanced his thinking skills are at ages eight and nine.

> "Studies show that better pretend play skills at age three and four are associated with better language skills at ages eight and nine."

Children on the autism spectrum can learn to pretend, but they need help. First of all, they must be ready to learn. When a child's functional play skills have developed to the point where he plays with several toys and can combine two or more "expected" play actions on a toy or toys (such as putting objects into the dumper of a truck, driving the truck along the floor and then dumping the objects onto the floor), he is ready to develop early pretend play.

Stages of Communication Development in Young Children with Autism

The four communication stages described below are used by The Hanen Centre in the More Than Words® Program to help parents of children with ASD become familiar with their child's stage of development. Because pretend play and communication development are connected, it is helpful to know whether your child's stage of communication shows he is ready to learn to pretend.

The four stages of communication development are:

Own agenda

The hallmark of this stage of communication is that the children are not yet sending messages to others intentionally. Parents have to figure out what their child wants or likes by paying close attention to what he is looking at, reaching for or smiling at. For example, a child at the Own Agenda stage might reach for the cookies on the counter top and move his body to try and get them. However, he has not yet figured out that he could send a message directly to his mother asking her to help him by looking at her or pulling her towards the cookies.

Requester

Children at the Requester stage have learned to send messages directly to others for the purpose of asking for things or rejecting them. They know that they need Mom or Dad's help to get what they want and they have learned to communicate with them in ways that achieve this goal. At the very early stages, Requesters do only one thing to send a message that does not include looking at another person. For example, they might pull their parent by the hand, taking them to the item they want, but looking only at the object. When Requesters get better at sending messages to ask for things, they start to combine different ways to send a message, including looking at the other person. For example, when a child sees cookies on the counter top, he looks at his mom and then back at the cookies while he reaches towards them. Now he is combining a look with an action (reaching) and this helps him check that the other person is attending to what he's attending to and knows what he wants.

Early Communicator

Like Requesters, children at the Early Communicator stage send messages to ask for and to reject things. However, they are also starting to communicate to connect socially with others. They now show objects, pictures, and events to others for the sole purpose of sharing their interests with someone else. These children also wait for others to respond when they do this. For example, a child points to a bus on the street, says "bus," and looks back to his Dad to make sure that he saw the bus as well. The boy waits for his father to look at the bus and say, "Yes, there's a bus!" Children at the Early Communicator stage are also starting to understand some questions and answer them appropriately. Later, they begin to ask others questions to gain information.

Partner

Children at the Partner stage communicate to ask for and reject things, as well as to connect socially with others. In addition, they are starting to have very short, early conversations with adults. These children are usually good at responding to what adults say to them, especially when they are asked questions. They might have a harder time responding when an adult makes a comment, not understanding that this requires some kind of response. They may not initiate their own ideas very often, however. Children at the Partner stage are starting to become interested in interacting with other children but have difficulty doing so.

Pretend Play, Stage of Communication and Joint Attention

Pretend play usually starts to emerge when children are at the Early Communicator stage. This is the stage when the child has developed **joint**

attention, which involves the ability to share attention with another person towards the same object or event. The purpose of sharing joint attention is social – it goes beyond just requesting. The child really wants to share the things he is interested in with someone. He may hold up a favourite toy to show it to a parent or he may point at a picture in a book and then look at his parent to make sure they see it too.

Mom shows Thomas the pretend bread by pointing to it. Thomas sees what she's pointing to and points to it as well. Now they're sharing their interest in the toy with each other.

Why is joint attention so important? Because it provides a basis for sharing experience that is essential for language development. If a child looks at something and points to it, the adult naturally talks about it, giving the child the words for what has captured his interest. The fact that the words the child hears are connected to what he is focused on make it easier and more motivating for him to learn from them. Joint attention is necessary when engaging in pretend play with another person because both players need to be able to attend to what the other person is saying and doing in order to build the play scenario cooperatively.

2

Your Child's Stage of Play and Next Steps in Pretend Play

Before you can start to help your child develop better pretend play skills, you need to identify his stage of play. In this section, you will identify whether your child is at the **functional**, **early pretend** or **later pretend** stage of play. Then you will use the checklist to decide on his next play step and how to help him get there.

Next Steps: Building Pretend Play for Children with Autism

While we know that pretend play can be challenging for children with autism, the good news is that these children *can* learn to pretend. The focus in this booklet is first on helping your child copy the pretend actions and ideas you show him and then learning to use these and other pretend ideas, including pretend sequences, on his own. Eventually, the goal is for him to create new ideas for pretend play on his own. All this is learned within fun, enjoyable interactions with you and other important people in his life.

In this section, you will:

1) identify your child's stage of pretend play; and
2) identify your child's next play step – this will be the step you will teach him

How Does Your Child Play?

Before you can start to help your child develop more advanced pretend play skills, you need to identify his stage of play.

Check the box beside the description that matches your child's most advanced level of play (the type of play becomes more advanced as you go down the list).

How My Child Plays

My child combines two or more "expected" play actions together. For example, he 1) places a car on top of a ramp; 2) pushes a lever to make the car go down the ramp; then 3) picks up the car and puts it back on the top of the ramp. ☐

My child pretends by using real-life objects or realistic miniature objects or toys in the way they were intended to be used. For example, he drinks from an empty cup or stirs a toy spoon in a toy pan. He usually does one action at a time. ☐

My child pretends by using real-life objects or realistic miniature objects or toys in the way they were intended to be used. He does more than one pretend play action at a time. For example, he stirs a toy spoon in a toy pan, then puts the spoon to the doll's mouth as if to feed her. Sometimes he even does three actions at a time. ☐

My child pretends by using an object as if it were a different object. For example, he uses a block as a car or a box as a house. ☐

My child pretends as if he were using an object when there is none. For example, he holds his fist to his ear and pretends to talk on the phone, but there is no object in his hand. ☐

If you said that your child...	Then your child is at the following stage of pretend play
combines two or more "expected" play actions together	**Multi-action functional stage**
pretends by using real-life objects or realistic miniature objects or toys in the way they were intended to be used (he may do one action or many actions with the toy)	**Early pretend stage**
pretends by using an object as if it were a different object or pretends as if he were using an object when there is none	**Later pretend stage**

Guidelines for Deciding on Next Steps for Pretend Play

There are some simple guidelines to help you choose the next step for your child as well as for choosing the best toys to help him learn that step.

Next steps for Multi-action Functional Players

If your child frequently combines two or more "expected" play actions together using many different kinds of toys...

His next play step is to:

- **pretend using real-life objects or realistic miniature objects or toys in the way they were intended to be used (early pretend stage of play)**

  To get your child on the road to early pretend play, aim to help him imitate some single pretend actions with real-life or realistic miniature toy objects. Because feeding, grooming and daily routines are so familiar to your child, these are the easiest ones for him to learn to pretend to do.

Objects and toys to use

Choose toys and objects for routines that your child enjoys. If he hates having his hair combed or washed, don't use those as pretend activities.

The most common pretend actions you could help your child learn are:

- Feeding – himself or a toy
  - using real cups, toy cups, cups with real straws, toy cups with miniature straws
  - using miniature toy utensils
  - using miniature food

- Cooking – using toys
  - using toy kitchen utensils, pots and pans etc.
- Bath-time activities
  - using a toy bath with doll, toy animals, cloth
- Shopping
  - using a toy shopping cart, pretend food, toy cash register
- Park
  - using miniature playground equipment (some doll sets have them)
- Doctor's kit
  - using a toy kit with a stethoscope, syringe, pill bottles, thermometer, blood pressure cuff, bandage, Band-Aids

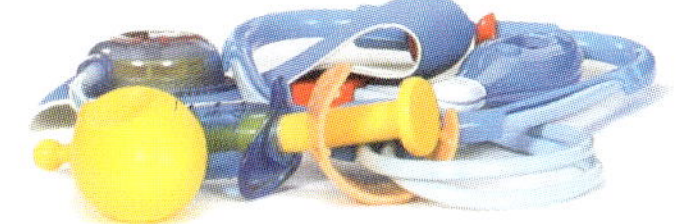

Next steps for Early Pretenders

There are two levels of early pretend play, and your child's next step depends on his level.

LEVEL 1	Your child pretends by acting on real-life objects or realistic miniature objects or toys in the way they were intended to be used using **one pretend play action at a time**.
LEVEL 2	Your child pretends by acting on real-life objects or realistic miniature objects or toys in the way they were intended to be used using **two or more** pretend play actions at a time.

LEVEL 1

If your child pretends by acting on real-life objects or realistic miniature objects or toys in the way they were intended to be used using **one pretend play action at a time**

His next play step is to:

- **Add to those pretend play actions so he creates a sequence of actions**

Toys and objects to use

When your child is ready to start adding to his single pretend actions to create a sequence, you will use the same toys and objects as you did before. However, you might need to add some toys to the activity. For example, if your child is really good at "feeding" himself and others with pretend food, you can add a wash cloth so he can learn to wipe the doll's hands and face after it has been fed or you can introduce toy knives and forks.

LEVEL 2

If your child pretends by acting on real-life objects or realistic miniature objects or toys in the way they were intended to be used using **two or more pretend play actions at a time**

His next play step is to…

- **Pretend by substituting one object for another; and**
- **Pretend with invisible objects (later pretend stage of play)**

In this case you will try to help your child learn both these types of later pretend play. He may find one kind of play easier than the other. You will find this out as you show him these two types of pretend play.

Toys and objects to use

You will start by using the same realistic toys and objects that you used during

Early Pretending. To help your child learn to use more advanced pretend play by substituting one object for another, start by substituting objects that look a little like the objects they are replacing. For example, a rectangular block could be a cell phone or a small box could be used as a cup.

You can move on to using objects that look nothing like the ones they are being substituted for as your child becomes used to more realistic objects in his pretend play. For example, if your child enjoys pretending to have a birthday party, you could have everyone who is playing wear party hats and have realistic looking presents to open. Then, you can pretend that a book is the birthday cake (a substitute that doesn't look much like the real object) and pretend to cut it. You can even combine using invisible items with substituted objects. For example, you could use a book as a birthday cake and pretend to light invisible candles on the cake and blow them out. You could also pretend to cut the cake and hand out invisible pieces.

An empty box could be a substitute for a pretend birthday cake.

Next steps for Later Pretenders

If your child pretends by substituting one object for another and pretends with invisible objects...

His next play step is to...

- **Expand on the pretend play that he is already doing**

Some things that you could help your child do include:

- come up with new ideas during the game that you have not done before

- take on a role and "act out" a situation – e.g., being a firefighter and saving you from a burning building or being a teacher who is giving you homework
- include other children in the pretend play that he is familiar with

Toys and objects to use

You will use a combination of realistic toys, invisible objects, and a variety of objects to represent something else. You can also use costumes to help your child take on his role. For example, if you and your child are pretending that he is a firefighter, you could get a firefighter hat or costume to dress in ahead of time. He might "drive" to the burning building in an invisible fire truck, and then use a long string as a hose to put the fire out.

3

Build Pretend Play Within Playful Interactions: Follow Your Child's Lead and R.O.C.K.

Play should always be fun for both you and your child. In this section, you will start out by learning how to follow your child's lead so he will want to play with you, rather than play alone. Using the 4Is (Include, Imitate, Interpret and Intrude), you will get your child involved in an enjoyable play interaction. Once you and he are having fun together, you can R.O.C.K. his play, and help him learn some new pretend play skills. R.O.C.K. involves showing your child a new kind of pretend play and encouraging him to copy it. The simple, yet powerful R.O.C.K. strategy helps you make learning to pretend easy and fun for your child. Once he has had lots of practice with the kind of pretend play you are teaching him, the goal is for him to use some new and creative pretend play all by himself.

What's Your Play Style?

How you act and talk with your child when you play and pretend together has an enormous effect on how your child plays and interacts with you. The more fun your child has when he plays with you, the more open he is to learning. A lot depends on your **play style**.

Take the "What's My Play Style?" quiz below to learn more about how you play with your child.

What's My Play Style?

R = Rarely S = Sometimes U = Usually

I decide what my child will play	R	S	U
I show or tell my child what to do or say when we play	R	S	U
I let my child choose the games we play and the objects/toys we play with	R	S	U
I get on the floor when I play with my child	R	S	U
I am playful and play like a "kid" with my child	R	S	U
I watch my child play from the sidelines	R	S	U
I play rough and tumble games (like chase and tag) with my child	R	S	U
I do quiet activities with my child (like board games or shape sorters)	R	S	U
I am animated and excited when I play with my child	R	S	U
I speak softly and stay calm when I play with my child	R	S	U

The Helper or Teacher style

If you said that you usually...

- decide what your child will play
- show or tell your child what to do or say when you play

...and rarely...

- let your child choose the objects, toys or games you play
- are playful and play like a "kid" with your child

... you likely have a Helper or Teacher style. While every parent needs to be a helper or teacher some of the time, if directing the play is how you ***usually*** interact with your child, then he is not getting enough opportunities to explore and experience the world in ways that interest him. Playing together might not be fun. It is also likely that he doesn't get enough opportunities to show you what he can do – and he might be able to do far more than you expect.

The Do Not Disturb style

If you said that you...

- rarely show or tell your child what to do or say when you play
- sometimes or usually watch your child play from the sidelines

... you likely have a Do Not Disturb style, which means that you let your child play alone, perhaps because he seems uninterested in playing with you. Some children with ASD need a calming influence since they can be overstimulated by what's going on around them. When a child seems overwhelmed by the noise or excitement of an activity, the Do Not Disturb parent style might be just the right fit at that moment.

But while all children need some time alone when they play, they also need to learn to play with others. Children on the autism spectrum learn a great deal when their parents get down on the floor and play with them, even if they seem unhappy about it at first.

The Cheerleader Style

If you said that you...

- usually decide what your child will play
- usually show or tell your child what to do or say when you play
- sometimes or usually get on the floor with your child
- sometimes or usually are playful and play like a "kid"
- sometimes or usually play rough and tumble games with your child
- sometimes or usually get very animated and get excited when you play with your child

... you likely have a Cheerleader style.

Parents with the Cheerleader style make the play exciting for their child. They are very expressive, using a loud voice and many gestures when they talk. They may get down on the floor, play rough and tumble games and get very animated. These kinds of parents are fun for children to be around.

Parents may use a Cheerleader style to encourage a child who is reluctant or passive to try something new. Some children need a very animated play partner to get them interested in playing.

However, in an effort to be a fun play partner, parents can overwhelm their child, especially one who is sensitive to loud sounds, and prevent him from playing with the things he's interested in. Being too animated, asking too many questions or giving too many directions can make your child feel pressured, making him less likely to want to play and communicate with you.

The Responsive style

If you said that you...

- usually let your child choose the games you play, as well as the objects/toys you play with
- rarely or sometimes show or tell your child what to do or say when you play
- usually get on the floor with your child
- sometimes or usually are playful and play like a "kid"
- sometimes are animated and excited when you play with your child
- sometimes speak softly and stay calm when you play with your child
- sometimes play rough and tumble games (like chase and tag) with your child
- sometimes do quiet activities with your child (like board games or shape sorters)

...you likely have a **Responsive style**. Parents with a Responsive style adapt the way they interact according to what their child is doing, feeling and communicating . They judge when to be calm and quiet, when to be the Cheerleader or somewhere in-between. They usually let their child choose what he plays and how he plays with it and they don't bombard him with questions or give a lot of directions.

Parents with a Responsive style also know that sometimes their child needs help in order to learn a new play skill. When that happens, they

provide direction for a while, helping him learn something new in an enjoyable, positive way. But they continue to encourage their child to interact and play with what interests him, building learning opportunities into these interactions all the time. Parents with a Responsive style are playful and they try to make sure that play time is always fun.

When building your child's pretend play, using a Responsive style will make all the difference in helping him stay involved in the play and learn more advanced play skills.

Before You Start to Play...

There are a few important things to do before you can start to play:

- **Identify your child's next play step in pretend play**
  If you skipped that section, go back to pages 20 – 26. You need a clear idea of the kind of pretend play you are helping your child learn before you start.
- **Get the toys ready** – Always use toys you know your child enjoys playing with.
- **Have your own toys** – Get your own toys so you never have to take your child's. Some of the toys should be the same as or similar to your child's.

Now you are ready to use two important strategies to build your child's pretend play:

- Follow your child's lead; and
- R.O.C.K. your child's pretend play

Following your child's lead helps you get involved with your child when he plays, making sure you include the things he enjoys. There is no teaching involved at this stage. You just become an equal play partner and have fun together.

R.O.C.K. your child's pretend play gives you the tools to teach him a new pretend play skill. It provides a simple and practical way to help your child take the next pretend play step.

Follow Your Child's Lead to Build Pretend Play

Following your child's lead during pretend play makes the play fun. When your child enjoys playing with you, he is motivated to interact and keep the play going. Learning also becomes a natural part of the interaction. This means that, to encourage and motivate your child to engage in pretend play, you have to make it more fun than playing alone.

There are two parts to following your child's lead:
First, you **Observe, Wait and Listen**
Then, you **follow your child's lead the 4I way**

Observe, Wait and Listen (OWL)

It all starts with **Observe**, **Wait** and **Listen**. You can never leave out this step because playing with your child means noticing and figuring out exactly what he's doing when he plays and what kind of play he enjoys. It also means giving him a chance to show you what he is interested in, as well as a chance to communicate with you.

Each letter of OWL offers an important guideline for what to do every time you play with your child.

Observe – and be face to face

The only way to get involved in your child's play is to take the time to see what he is doing and exactly what he is interested in. Watch closely in silence. Notice the toys he plays with and what he does with them. If he is playing with a truck, you may see that what really interests him is making the truck hit a wall. Or he may be playing with a doll, but what has really grabbed his attention is how the doll's hair feels when he touches it.

When you observe your child, get down so you are face to face. You may need to get onto the floor and lie on your side or stomach to get face to face. Or you may need to sit on the floor if your child is sitting at a little table. Just be sure that you and your child can look into each others' eyes without having to look up or down.

Observing is a key step to helping your child develop more advanced play skills. It allows you to become very aware of all the things your child does when he plays. It also allows you to pick up any subtle attempts to interact with you like a quick look at you or a push of a toy in your direction.

Wait

Waiting can be very difficult at first because it may require a change from the way you usually interact with your child. You may feel that you need to help him, tell him what to do or ask him to name an object. While there is a lot you can do to help your child progress in his play skills, the best way to start is by waiting and letting him play the way he wants to play.

When you wait, get close to your child, look interested and don't say anything at all. Just by waiting, you send your child a very powerful message. You are telling him that he can choose what he wants to do, without any suggestions or directions from you. You are also giving him the time and space to communicate with you, which he might not get otherwise.

If waiting is hard for you (and it is for most people), count to five or even to 10 to remind yourself to stay silent. Once your child starts to play or communicates with you, respond immediately, showing your interest.

Mom waits to give Lili a chance to play the way *she* wants to play.

Listen

Listening goes hand in hand with observing and waiting. It is the last part of a strategy designed to give your child the chance to follow his interests and communicate with you when he is ready. As with observing and waiting, listening means staying quiet and paying close attention to your child as he plays. If he says something or makes a sound, it is important to listen carefully so you can respond immediately and show that you are interested. Being listened to makes your child feel important and encourages him to communicate again.

> “Being listened to makes your child feel important and encourages him to communicate again.”

Listening is very helpful when your child uses echolalia (i.e., imitates or "parrots" the words or phrases he's heard other people say.) If you listen to the tone of your child's echoes, you learn a lot about the meaning of what he's saying. For example, if you ask, "Do you want to make a fruit salad?" and he repeats your question exactly as you said it with the same upward questioning intonation, it may mean he doesn't understand you. If, however, he repeats what you say and changes the intonation as if making a statement, he's probably saying, "Yes, I want to make a fruit salad."

Follow your child's lead the 4I way

The goal of following your child's lead is to get an interaction going and keep it going. By following his lead, you let him know that you're interested in what he's doing and that you're joining in the play as an equal partner. This is very motivating for him, and you will notice him paying more attention to you and interacting with you for longer periods of time.

The main guideline to following your child's lead is to stick with what he is interested in. Even if your child isn't actually interacting with you, you can still include his interests by getting involved in what he is doing.

It is much easier for your child to interact when you follow his lead because you are building on what he is already thinking about. So don't ask him to do something different with his toys or attend to or play with something else, even if you think it will be fun. Don't tell him what to do or ask him questions. The idea is to make the interaction as positive as possible so that he will want to stay involved with you.

There are four "I" steps to following your child's lead during play:

- **I**nclude your child's interests
- **I**nterpret
- **I**mitate
  and
- **I**ntrude

Include your child's interests

Including your child's interests is something you do every time you play with your child. All the strategies that follow are built on this important strategy. When you join in with what your child is doing, choose toys that your child wants to play with and keep playing the game the way *he* wants to.

Follow these steps to use this strategy effectively:

FIRST...

- **imitate** what your child is doing (use your own toy so you don't take your child's) (**imitating** is discussed in more detail below)

  OR

- **help your child do what he is doing** by handing him the pieces of the game

THEN...

- **comment** on what your child has done and **point** to it, making it sound exciting

For example:

If your child puts pretend food into a toy grocery cart and heads towards the cash register, **include his interests** by:

- **imitating him** – get your own pretend food and put it into the cart; and
- **commenting** and pointing – for example, "You got the apples! Yummy! I got some French fries."

Or

- **helping him in his play** – hand him different foods for him to put into his cart; and
- **commenting** – for example, "Everybody loves pizza!"

Important tips for commenting

- **Comment as quickly as possible** so the information your child hears is connected to what's happening at that very moment.
- **Keep what you say short and simple**, but always use good grammar. For example, when your child puts a doll into a toy bath, instead of saying, "Baby in bath", add the little words that make sentence grammatical – i.e. "The baby's in the bath."
- **Use your child's words** – Your child will feel empowered if your comment includes some of the words he has used. For example, if he is making a toy firefighter put out a "fire" and says, "Get the hose", you can say, "Okay, let's get the hose and spray the water."

Interpret

When playing with your child, you may find that he sends you messages without using words or using just one or two words. When this happens, he needs to hear models of the words he could say. You do this when you interpret or 'Say it as he would if he could'. This means that you use the words you think your child would say if he were able to. For example, if you are playing with a doctor's kit and your child puts a miniature syringe to your arm and says "Arm," you should give your child a model of the words he could use. When you do, say exactly what he would say – i.e., "I'm giving you a needle." In time, your child might repeat your model. It is especially important to interpret from the child's perspective when he is using echolalia. Children who repeat exactly what is said to them need to learn to repeat the words they *should* be saying.

Imitate

Imitating your child during play is a powerful strategy. It is very exciting for him when you copy his actions, sounds and words. It shows that you are interested in what he is doing and accepting of his play. This gets his attention and makes him more interested in interacting with you. The result is longer, back and forth interactions that are great fun for you both. And when you imitate your child when he plays, he may imitate you back, making imitation an enjoyable part of your interactions. This lays the foundation for using imitation to help your child learn new play skills.

"When you imitate your child when he plays, he may imitate you back, making imitation an enjoyable part of your interactions."

Remember that when you imitate your child's actions with a toy, you should never take his toy! Make sure you have a toy that's the same as (or similar to) his.

Intrude

Sometimes, you may observe, wait and listen and follow your child's lead by including, imitating and commenting, but your child may not respond or may keep doing what he's doing, ignoring you. In this case, you need to do something different, something that will get his attention in a fun, playful way. You need to **intrude**. This means insisting on joining in on what your child is doing, even if he doesn't want you to.

Eric is so absorbed in moving his toy truck back and forth, he's taking no notice of Mom's efforts to join in the play. So Mom intrudes by bringing out his stuffed dog. She bounces it up and down on Eric's leg and says animatedly, "Mr. Dog wants to take a ride on your firetruck!"

The best way to Intrude with children who are playing with a toy in the same way over and over is to **add something new to the game**. For example, a child is sitting with a pile of foam letters, picking one up at a time and naming it, then putting it down before starting again with another. Mom points to each letter and labels it. The child looks at his Mom and smiles but continues playing with the letters his way. So Mom gets a puppet and playfully makes the puppet "eat" each letter after the child picks it up. At first, the child resists this new game and ignores the puppet. Mom persists, and stays animated and playful. The child starts to smile at the puppet "eating" the letters and then begins to "feed" the letters to the puppet himself.

Often, you will be able to intrude by **redirecting your child** to the model of pretending that you would like him to learn. For example, your child is good at "feeding" others and you want to teach him a sequence of cooking the food before he feeds it to the dolls. While he is feeding the dolls repetitively, you can get his attention by saying his name and suggesting that he cook the food first. Point to the "kitchen" until he looks at it. You are now ready to teach him how to do something he has never done before.

> "Intruding breaks the cycle of your child's difficulty with interaction and allows you to work your way into his play."

Intruding breaks the cycle of your child's difficulty with interaction and allows you to work your way into his play, even if he seems not to welcome it at first. Once you have established an interaction, you can move on to helping him learn to play with R.O.C.K.

ROCK Your Child's Pretend Play

You have gotten the interaction going by following your child's lead using the 4I's: you have **included your child's interests**, **interpreted** his messages, **imitated** his actions, sounds and words and, when necessary, **intruded** playfully so you could join in on his play and interact with him.

Now that your child is enjoying the interaction, smiling and paying attention to you and what you are doing with the toys, he is ready to learn some new pretend play skills with R.O.C.K.. When you R.O.C.K. your child's pretend play, you are helping him learn to use more advanced forms of pretend play in a fun, interesting way.

R	**Repeat the pretend action/s you want your child to learn**
O	Wait to give your child the **Opportunity** to copy your pretend action/s
C	**Cue** your child if you need to (if he doesn't copy your pretend actions)
K	**Keep the play going** and, once he's learned to do the pretend action/s, **Keep it changing**

Once again, review your child's next step in pretend play before you start to R.O.C.K. his play.

Repeat the pretend action/s you want your child to learn – *Show your child the pretend action. You might need to repeat it more than once, especially if it is a new play situation for him.*

Model the new pretend play action you want your child to learn (his next play step) and comment on what you have done, pointing to the toy. For example, if you are pretending to wash a toy lion in a miniature bath tub, say, "I'm washing the lion! Look, he's so clean!" and point to the toy lion. You may need to do this more than once.

Mom models pretending with an invisible object (a cell phone) and says, "Hi Daddy! I'm playing with Eric."

Wait to give your child the Opportunity to copy your pretend action/s
– Your child needs a few seconds to process what he has seen and heard before he responds. So give him some time – stop playing and wait to see what he does.

When you wait to give your child the opportunity to copy your pretend action, he may do so. In that case, skip to **Keep it going**. Repeat the pretend action, comment on it and point to the toy or object, showing your excitement. Then wait again.

If he does nothing or continues to play with the objects as he was doing before, then you will need to give him a cue.

Cue your child if you need to
– Your child may need extra help to copy your pretend action since it is so new to him. Cues let your child know what to do and are an important part of helping him learn how to play.

If your child doesn't copy the pretend play step, there are four types of cues you can give him to help him learn how to play. Start with expectant waiting for at least 5 seconds. If he needs a stronger cue, choose one from the three below, starting with the first one, which is the least intrusive. Move on to the others if he needs more help:

Cues to use if waiting expectantly doesn't work:

- First... **show him the pretend action again and comment on it** – for example, "I'm washing the lion in the bathtub. He's dirty so I am washing him."
- If showing doesn't work, **tell him how to do the action and point** – for example, "Wash the lion. Use your cloth and wipe his face" (as she points to the cloth so he will know to pick it up).
- If telling him what to do doesn't work, **use hand over hand modelling** – take your child's hands and move them so he performs the pretend action with the toy, describing what he is doing. For example, as you give him the cloth and move his hands in a washing motion over the toy lion, say, "You're washing the lion."

Your goal is for your child to imitate you without cues. So, remember to **wait each time you model the new play step** so that, when he can copy it all by himself, you give him an opportunity to do that.

Once your child has copied the new pretend play step, with or without a cue, go to **Keep it going**.

Keep the play going and Keep it changing!
– It's always important to keep the play going so your child is interacting with you and having many opportunities to learn pretend play. It is also important to change the pretend and show your child more advanced kinds of pretend play once he has made good progress.

Keep the play going

Keep the interaction going so your child continues to have opportunities to learn from you.

If your child seems to be losing interest in the play, ask yourself:

- Am I still **including** his interests?
- If his attention strays, ask yourself if you need to **imitate** him again to get his attention.
- If you lose him and he moves on to something else, you may need to **intrude** – get face to face and redirect him back to the play so he starts to interact with you again.

Keep the play changing

Once your child has learned the pretend play steps and is using them often, keep the play changing so he continues to learn.

You can change the play by:

- Adding new toys
- Showing your child a new pretend play step if he is using the one you are teaching consistently and with many different toys (review page 20 - 21 to see if your child is ready for a new play step)

4

Real Life Examples

Now let's look at how this works in real life. Lili and Eric's parents are following their child's lead and using R.O.C.K. to help them take the next step in pretend play. Lili and Eric are having so much fun, they don't realize that they are learning new ways to pretend, that will help them develop more advanced language, social and problem-solving skills.

ROCKing Lili's Pretend Play

The Functional Player learns early pretend play

Mom has to identify Lili's stage of play before she can decide on her next play step.

FIRST... **Mom observes Lili when she is playing with toys in order to identify her stage of play:**

She sees that Lili combines two or more "expected" actions on a toy. For example, she puts plastic coins into a slot in her toy cash register, pushes the button that makes the coins drop into the drawer, then turns the handle to open the drawer and takes the coins out. She also attaches Lego blocks to the back of a Lego tractor, puts a man in the seat of the tractor and drives it along the floor.

Lili is at the **multi-action functional** stage of play.

SECOND... **Mom identifies Lili's next pretend play step and the toys she needs:**

Mom decides that Lili's next play step is to start to **pretend using real-life objects or realistic miniature objects, doing one action at a time** (early pretend play).

Since Lili has a favourite bear that she likes to carry around, Mom decides to use the bear to help her learn to pretend.

The best toys to use to help Lili learn early pretend play: Mom gets another toy bear, as well as some toy food.

THEN... **Mom Follows Lili's lead**

When Lili picks up her bear, Mom has her own bear ready so she can join in the play and get Lili's attention. Mom picks up her bear and carries it so Lili can see what she is doing. Lili notices right away and Mom says "Look, we both have bears," pointing to each one. Lili looks at her bear and repeats, "Bear." The interaction is established so Mom decides she can start to teach her to pretend.

THEN... **Mom R.O.C.K.s Lili's play:**

Repeat the pretend action

Mom decides that the pretend play action she will show Lili will be to feed the bear a toy doughnut. She models feeding the bear by putting the doughnut up to the bear's mouth. She says, "Mr. Bear is hungry. I'm giving him some food." Then she says, "Your bear is also hungry" and gives Lili the toy doughnut.

Mom models feeding the bear by putting the doughnut up to the bear's mouth and making a comment.

Give the Opportunity to copy the pretend action/s

Then Mom waits to give Lili a chance to pretend to feed the bear. She waits for about 10 seconds, but Lili makes no move to feed him.

Cue

Lili needs more help to copy Mom's pretend actions, so Mom repeats the action and says, "Mr. Bear is hungry. I'm giving him some food," as she pretends to feed the bear. "Give Mr. Bear some food," she says, pointing to the doughnut and then to the bear. But Lili just holds the doughnut, not extending her hand to the bear's mouth.

This time, Mom's cue is more direct. "Put the doughnut in Mr. Bear's mouth. The bear wants to eat," she says. She points to the doughnut again.

This time, Lili takes the doughnut and pretends to feed the bear.

Mom says, "You're feeding Mr. Bear. He likes that doughnut. Yum yum."

K Keep the play going

Lili needs lots of practice now that she has started to use early pretend play. So Mom keeps the play going by showing her how to feed the bear other realistic-looking toy foods, as well as giving the bear a drink from a toy cup. Lili got that one quickly. Mom also gives Lili practice on many different toy animals. After lots of repetition, Lili doesn't need cues. Mom just has to wait after she models the pretend feeding, offering Lili an opportunity to copy her. And she does, every time. Lili even learns to imitate feeding dolls and animals using toy utensils – *e.g.*, using a toy spoon to feed a doll soup or cereal and a toy fork to feed meat and vegetables.

Mom keeps the play going by modelling a new pretend action: giving the bear a drink. It doesn't take long for Lili to imitate that action.

...and Once Lili has learned to do the pretend action/s, Keep it changing

When Lili is feeding toys all by herself, Mom can now change the kind of pretend she is showing her. She adds some new single pretend actions to the mix:

- Cooking – Mom models stirring "soup" in a pot on the toy stove, saying, "We are going to have some soup. I'm waiting for it to get hot!"
- Drinking tea – mom models drinking from a cup, saying "Mmm... this tea is my favourite!" or "Uh-oh, I need some more milk in my tea."
- Bathing dolls – Mom models putting a baby in a toy bathtub and washing it with a small cloth, saying, "Let's wash the baby."

Once Lili has shown that she can pretend to feed herself and others, Mom can add to the feeding activity in order to create a pretend play sequence. She can start by teaching her to "cook" the food before she feeds it to the dolls. Once Lili is able to do both "cooking" and "feeding" on her own, Mom should add another step, such as cleaning up afterwards by wiping everyone's hands and face with a cloth.

At this point, Lili is only able to pretend in one kind of activity – feeding her toys. To further build her pretend play, Mom should focus on teaching her other activities in which she could pretend, starting with single pretend actions. For example, she might teach Lili to wash the bear's hair in a miniature bathtub or to put groceries in a shopping cart.

ROCKing Eric's Pretend Play

The Early Pretend Player learns later pretend play

Mom has to identify Eric's stage of play before she can decide on his next play step.

FIRST... **Mom Observes Eric when he is playing with toys so she can identify his stage of play**

Mom observes that Eric is good at pretending in many different activities using miniature or realistic objects, as well as invisible objects. He pretends to be the doctor, taking Mom's temperature and giving her a bandage. He also pretends to cook in the toy kitchen and then feeds others, and he uses the toy bus to take his animals and dolls to school.

Eric is at the **early pretend** stage of play.

SECOND... **Mom identifies Eric's next pretend play step and the toys he needs**

Mom decides that Eric's next play step is to **start to pretend by substituting one object for another** within a pretend play sequence he is already familiar with. Because he really enjoys being the "doctor", Mom decides to use some pieces of the doctor's kit but replaces the pretend bandages with a roll of tape ahead of time.

THEN... **Mom Follows Eric's lead**

Mom sees Eric playing with his favourite toy animal. He is pretending that the lion is drinking tea using a miniature tea set. Mom gets her own toy animal, a stuffed puppy dog, as well as a tea cup and the doctor's kit, and sits across from Eric. She starts to **imitate** him by feeding her dog some tea and making comments about what is happening, saying, "Mmm, the lion and the dog love tea!" Then she adds something new to the game. She pretends that her dog has fallen down and hurt his knee. "Ouch", she says, "I hurt my knee! I need to see a doctor!" Eric watches this and starts to touch Mom's dog to try and make him feel better.

Mom now has Eric's attention and is ready to teach him a new way to pretend.

THEN... **Mom R.O.C.K.s Eric's play**

Repeat the pretend action

Mom puts the dog on a little chair in front of her and Eric. She takes out the doctor's kit and uses the miniature thermometer to take the dog's temperature. Then she takes out the tape from the doctor's kit and says, "Here is a bandage to put on the dog's knee." She places the roll of tape over the dog's knee and says, "I'm putting a bandage on his knee. Now he feels better."

Mom models substituting one object for another. She uses a roll of tape as a substitute for a bandage, placing it on the dog's "sore" knee.

Give the Opportunity to copy the pretend action/s

Mom now holds out the roll of tape and waits for Eric to take it from her. She waits for 5 seconds, but Eric does not take the tape. Instead, he has a confused look on his face.

Cue

Eric needs more help to copy Mom's pretend actions. Mom puts the tape on the dog's knee again, saying to the dog, "Here's another bandage to help your knee feel better." Then Mom gives Eric a more direct cue. She holds out the roll of tape and says "Here Eric, the dog needs another bandage. Take it and put it on his knee." She points to the dog's knee with her other hand.

Eric takes the bandage and puts it on the dog's knee. Mom says, "You put the bandage on the dog! He feels so much better now."

Once Mom gives Eric a clear cue, Eric knows what to do. He lifts the dog's leg and starts to put the tape on the dog's knee.

K Keep the play going

Mom knows she has to give Eric lots more practice substituting one object for another in different activities. She uses R.O.C.K. to teach him to imagine that an object is something quite different from what it actually is in real life. She does this by using a banana as a phone to call Grandma and say "hi", and by pretending that pebbles are coins to pay for things at a pretend grocery store.

...and once Eric has learned to do the pretend action/s, Keep it changing

When Eric is able to pretend easily by substituting one object for another in many different play situations, it is time to expand on the pretend play that he is already doing.

Mom decides to introduce Eric to taking on the role of another person within pretend play. She decides to use the "doctor" scenario that he is already comfortable with. To help Eric take on the role of being a doctor, she will give him some props, including a doctor's coat and a toy stethoscope. Then she will model some of the phrases that a doctor would say, such as "What seems to be the problem today?" and "Get some rest and you'll feel better soon."

As she plays "doctor" with Eric, Mom will continue to model how a doctor talks and behaves. By acting out what a doctor would do and say throughout the game, Eric will learn to see things from another person's perspective. This will help him interact more effectively with others in many different situations, including during interactions with his peers.

Looking Back

While children on the autism spectrum don't often pretend on their own, they can learn to engage in this type of play – and have lots of fun doing it. You can help your child develop pretend play skills by first identifying his current stage of play and then figuring out his next steps. Then, you **Observe**, **Wait** and **Listen** to your child so you can see what he is interested in. This enables you to **Follow Your Child's Lead** with the 4 Is: **Include**, **Interpret**, **Imitate** and **Intrude**. These 4 ways of following your child's lead help you get your child involved in a fun, back and forth playful interaction, that involves doing what he enjoys most. Then, you follow the **R.O.C.K.** strategy which gives you a clear structure for showing your child how to move on to the next step in pretend play.

R.O.C.K. also provides you with ideas for expanding newly-learned pretend play skills to new toys and new activities. In time, your child will take these ideas and start to pretend on his own. By helping your child develop a repertoire of pretend play skills, you are building his social, language and thinking skills and giving him the tools to play with other children.

References

For a complete list of references, visit www.hanen.org/MakePlayROCK-references

Sample

Sample Pretend Play Plan
(see pages 20-21 for a description of the stages)

My child is at the following stage of pretend play: Early Pretend

The next pretend play step for my child is to: Pretend using invisible objects (later pretend play)

My child enjoys playing with the following toys or objects: She likes pretending to brush her doll's hair, clean her teeth and wash her face with realistic objects

My child can achieve his/her next play step by learning to imitate the following pretend actions/s: Brush her doll's hair with an invisible brush

What I will do first...

When my child is playing with a toy/objects, I will:

- Get down on the floor so we are face to face
- Put the toy/s I plan to use beside me, along with some duplicates or similar toys
- **O**bserve what s/he is doing with the toy/s
- **W**ait to see what else s/he will do or communicate; and
- **L**isten for any sounds or words

Then I will **Include my child's interests** by:

- **imitating** what my child is doing (using my own toy)
- **helping my child do what s/he is doing** by handing him/her the pieces of the game
- **commenting** on what I have done and **pointing** to it, making it sound exciting
- **Interpreting** what my child has communicated

If I can't get my child to attend to what I am doing, I will **Intrude**

Then, I will R.O.C.K. my child's play...

– I will **Repeat** the pretend actions/s I want my child to learn.

When s/he does the following actions with toys/objects: pretends to brush her doll's hair with a toy brush

I will **model** the following pretend action: I will pretend to brush my doll's hair with an invisible brush

I will **point** to the toy (even if invisible) and **comment** on what I have done by saying: I'm brushing her hair. She looks so pretty.

– I will **Offer** my child an **Opportunity** to copy my pretend action/s.
I will wait for at least 5-10 seconds

– I will **Cue** my child if s/he doesn't imitate the pretend actions I have modelled for him/her.

The first cue will be: I will say, "Here's the brush," (as I "hand" it to her). "Brush your dolly's hair."

If that doesn't work, I will try the following cue:
I will give her some physical help. I will move her hand over the doll's hair as if she is brushing it

– **Keep** the play going *and* **Keep** it changing!

Once my child has imitated the pretend play step, I will keep the game going by:
Adding new invisible objects to the play, like an invisible toothbrush and face cloth and using R.O.C.K. to help her learn these pretend actions, like I did with brushing the doll's hair.

Once my child can easily imitate or do the pretend play action on his/her own, I will keep the game changing by: Using invisible objects in different pretend activities such as feeding her dolls and other stuffed animals with an invisible spoon and bowls or cooking a meal with an invisible spoon and pots on an invisible stove.

My Child's Pretend Play Plan
(see pages 20-21 for a description of the stages)

My child is at the following stage of pretend play: ____________________

The next pretend play step for my child is to: ____________________

____

My child enjoys playing with the following toys or objects: ____________________

____

My child can achieve his/her next play step by learning to imitate the following pretend actions/s: ____________________

What I will do first...

When my child is playing with a toy/objects, I will:

- Get down on the floor so we are face to face
- Put the toy/s I plan to use beside me, along with some duplicates or similar toys
- **O**bserve what s/he is doing with the toy/s
- **W**ait to see what else s/he will do or communicate; and
- **L**isten for any sounds or words

Then I will **Include my child's interests** by:

- **imitating** what my child is doing (using my own toy)
- **helping my child do what s/he is doing** by handing him/her the pieces of the game
- **commenting** on what I have done and **pointing** to it, making it sound exciting
- **Interpreting** what my child has communicated

If I can't get my child to attend to what I am doing, I will **Intrude**

Then, I will R.O.C.K. my child's play...

R – I will **Repeat** the pretend actions/s I want my child to learn.

When s/he does the following actions with toys/objects: ____________________

____

© Hanen Early Language Program, 2015.
This Pretend Play Plan is from the Hanen guidebook *Put Pretending into Your Child's Play* (Weitzman & Drake, 2015) and may be copied for personal use only.

I will **model** the following pretend action: ______________________________

____

I will **point** to the toy (even if invisible) and **comment** on what I have done by saying:

____

O – I will **Offer** my child an **Opportunity** to copy my pretend action/s.

I will wait for at least ________ seconds

C – I will **Cue** my child if s/he doesn't imitate the pretend actions I have modelled for him/her.

The first cue will be: ______________________________

____

If that doesn't work, I will try the following cue:

____

____

K – **Keep** the play going *and* **Keep** it changing!

Once my child has imitated the pretend play step, I will keep the game going by:

____

____

____

Once my child can easily imitate or do the pretend play action on his/her own, I will keep the game changing by: ______________________________

____

____

© Hanen Early Language Program, 2015.
This Pretend Play Plan is from the Hanen guidebook *Put Pretending into Your Child's Play* (Weitzman & Drake, 2015) and may be copied for personal use only.